My Small World

Anshu Prasad

Made with ❤ on the BookLeaf Publishing Platform

www.bookleafpub.in

www.bookleafpub.com

Dedication

This book is dedicated to my family and friends, who fill my life with love, laughter, and endless inspiration. To my parents, thank you for always encouraging me to follow my dreams and for believing in me even when I doubted myself. To my friends, thank you for the fun times, the shared secrets, and the memories that make my heart smile.

I also want to dedicate this collection to all the young dreamers out there. May you always find the courage to express yourself and the joy in discovering the beauty of the world around you. Keep dreaming, keep writing, and never stop believing in the magic of your own words.

Preface

Hi there! My name is Anshu Prasad, and I'm just 11 years old. This collection of poems is a little piece of my world that I want to share with you. Writing poetry is like opening a window to my heart and letting the words fly out like butterflies. Each poem is a snapshot of my thoughts, feelings, and the things I see around me every day.

In these pages, you'll find poems about the simple joys of life, like playing with friends, the beauty of nature, and the magic of dreams. You'll also read about the moments that make me think deeply, like when I see someone sad or when I wonder about the future. Sometimes, the world can be a big and confusing place, but writing helps me make sense of it all.

I hope that as you read these poems, you'll feel a connection to the things that matter most to you. Maybe you'll remember your own childhood adventures or find comfort in knowing that someone else feels the same way you do.
Thank you for taking the time to read my poems. I hope they bring a smile to your face and a little bit of wonder to your heart.

Acknowledgements

I would like to express my heartfelt gratitude to everyone who has supported me on this journey of writing and creating.
To my parents, thank you for your endless love, encouragement, and for always being my biggest cheerleaders. Your belief in me has given me the confidence to share my words with the world.

To my teachers, thank you for nurturing my love for writing and for inspiring me to explore the beauty of language. Your guidance has been invaluable.

To my friends, thank you for the laughter, the adventures, and for always being there to listen to my poems. Your friendship means the world to me.

A special thank to my family, for your wisdom, patience, and for helping me grow as a writer. Your support has been a guiding light.

Lastly, to all the readers, thank you for taking the time to read my poems. Your appreciation and feedback are what make this journey so rewarding.

1. My School

This school is so- so nice
They will get you ready for exams in a trice
This school is So-so nice
They even win every prize

They are good not to make us fight
They work like this day and night
They make us do our rights
And make us students futures very bright

This school is the best of all
They will not let you fall

If you have fears,
Do not worry!
Your teachers are here 😊

This school has a good hue
I am happy you are still here too
My School is the best school ..!

2. My Wonderful 2024

The year 2024 was a nice delight,
It was nice to see my friends so bright!
We will all save this year like a file,
Like a delicate, beautiful tile

The field trip was nice to be around,
As I went to the top of the rock wall and didn't want to
come down!
We danced and danced the whole day,
I didn't want the day to go away!

The math day was a pleasure,
It was a real treasure!
Of many topics together,
I would love math forever!

The annual day was a spectacular feat,
As all the dancers got on their feet
It was very nice to get a glance
To see my BFF Dance!

But now, we have to say Adios
To the friends we love the most
It was very nice to move forward
And to remember this Flashback!

3. My Aunt

My Aunt acts like a teacher
And a preacher ..!

A few days back was her birthday
And we made it a special one .!

She was said to be the mischievous one of all
Yet she was disciplined when she was small
My Aunt is a bodacious dude
Bodacious enough to fix a Feud .!

My aunt is fun and exciting
Even more when celebrating :) ,
Oh .! dear aunty we love you so
We love you from head to Toe ..!

4. A sport that I ..

.... love is Badminton

I love the sport that i play
But trust me it might look easy
But its hard as learning Latin..

I Love Badminton because of its Out's and IN's
As only one player Win's
The matches are way too exciting
as if retrograde is aligning

Badminton will always be a spectacular sport
Its a change in my life of some sort
Badminton will live in the heart of all
As i always listen to its call ..!

5. Our Nutrients

All the food we eat
like all the grains , rice and wheat
but there are a few nutrients
i'll be happy to get into addictions ..

Carb's are energy giving
as we will do things fast and get back to our living .
vitamins and minerals are a curiosity
but they help to build immunity..!

proteins are used by body builders
if they dont have their shakes , they become tilters ;) ..!
Fats must be taken in small amount
to keep a progressive health account ....

In every bite, life's essence flows, Nutrients nourish, as nature bestows...

6. When I fly my paper plane

When I fly my paper plane
It looks as nice as floating down a garden lane
when i learned to fly my plane, Joy and wonder, I did
gain.
In the sky, it dances free, a simple pleasure, just for me.
With each glide, my heart takes flight, soaring high, a
pure delight.

Every time I try everyday
It keeps on soaring day by day
When i fly it into the air
Everyday someone will catch it and put it in their lair

When ever i fly it on a hill
It'll fly and fly and get struck in a windmill

But what will you choose ?
To Soar
Or to walk like a Boar..

7. Dear Dairy

My dear dairy ,

You hold my feelings very tight
and we will show me the light
Few things are read and blue ,
you have a very good hue

Sunflowers are yellow ,
Tulips are purple
You are like a yummy Truffle ,
capturing all my Huffel , puffle and struggle ..

8. Our Mistakes

Mistakes are lessons not failures
we are all not perfect as we are
Dont become a failure
but being perfect is hard

Once i tried to be perfectly good
But then the trail di not go as planned ,
I wanted to fix everything If i could
But for me being perfect is banned

I might look perfect as I'm not
with all of my accomplishments and everything
but when it comes to being perfect
I barely win everything ..!

9. Our Universe

Our universe is the milky way
However other planets are far away
But i know a little something of each planet
so come join me in this universe adventure

Mercury if close to the light , its hot in the day but cold
in the night
Venus is the hottest pot , you will sweat as you will feel
very hot .!
Earth gives birth to life, for everyone to live and thrive
Mars is like a Red mallet, as it is called the red planet
On Jupiter you will feel very small, as it is big and has
more moons than all .!
Saturn is the prettiest , with its ring shining bright
Uranus will get a hold, for the planet who survives the
cold
Neptune will blow you away , with all his heavy winds
he sways
Pluto is sad to know that this planet is is more..

Here is our Universe , do we have any other meta-verse??

11

10. Grandma - My Ajji

Ajji , today is your special day, you are as sweet as bajji ,

A journey of love, laughter, and cheers. Your heart is a treasure, so warm and kind, A more wonderful soul, we could never find.
Through the seasons of life, you've been our guide, With wisdom and grace, always by our side. Your stories and smiles, a comforting light, In your presence, everything feels just right.

You've nurtured and cared with hands so gentle, Your love is a gift, so fundamental. On this special day, we celebrate you, With gratitude and joy, our hearts are true.

May your days be filled with happiness and cheer, Surrounded by loved ones, year after year. For in our hearts, you hold a special place, A beacon of love, an endless embrace.

Happy birthday, Grandma, seventy-five years strong,
With love and blessings, we sing this song. May your life
be bright, your heart be light, A celebration of you, our
shining light.

11. Forests

A forest is a great place to be
with all the animals and trees
But then why do we pollute it
it is really a mystery

The weaver bird weaves nests
and it is as pretty as so
The OX is the strongest
they work by saying heave - ho!

We can all grow our own forest
this is our part
But those who build industries
Will not take this to heart

12. Peace

All i want are no fights
as i can help
By showing people the light

You can give flowers
or a chocolate box
As they give a power
for a little love

Or you can apologize
And say sorry
As it holds a promise
Without any worry

13. Girls ..

Girls are the best ,
there is no doubt
boys are the goofy ones
for them everything is loose-ons

girls can most do everything
boys struggle with little things

my dear Bro , i am just joking
both are super-ior
but , dont blame me ..
as girls are the real souvenirs :)

14. My MOM

My mom is Chaitra, her sister is Megha, My mom is the
best, so is her mom Veda.
Mom multitasks, helping me study, Without even asking,
she does things so ready.
My mom is always above, like she has a magical glove,
She is as soft as a dove, healing everyone with her love.
Mom's love is endless, her care is profound, In her
embrace, comfort is always found.
She juggles tasks with grace and ease, Her dedication
and love never cease.
With a heart so pure and a spirit so bright, She fills our
days with warmth and light.
Mom, you're a treasure, a gift from above, Thank you for
your endless love.

15. My Struggles

In the world of a ten-year-old, life can be tough,
Navigating through days, sometimes feeling rough. With
school and homework, the pressure is high, Trying to
keep up, reaching for the sky.
Early mornings, rushing out the door, Backpack heavy,
feet on the floor. Lessons to learn, tests to take, Dreams
to chase, goals to make.
Friendships to build, sometimes they break, Heartaches
and joys, decisions to make. Balancing playtime with
chores at home, Finding a space where they can roam.
Parents' expectations, teachers' demands, Trying to
understand life's commands. Feeling small in a world so
vast, Hoping each struggle will soon be past.
But amidst the challenges, there's a light, A spirit so
strong, ready to fight. With resilience and courage, they
stand tall, A ten-year-old's journey, conquering it all.
Through ups and downs, they find their way, Growing
stronger with each passing day. For in their heart, a fire
burns bright, A ten-year-old's struggle, a beautiful sight.

16. From a Kid to a Tween

From kid to tween, a journey so grand, A world of
changes, a new life at hand.
Leaving behind the toys and games, Embracing new
challenges, new aims.
No more simple days of carefree play, Homework and
projects now fill the day.
Friendships grow deeper, emotions run high, Navigating
feelings, learning to fly.

Exploring new interests, discovering dreams, Life's a bit
more complex, or so it seems.
Balancing schoolwork with fun and friends, A tween's
adventure never ends.
Growing taller, stronger, and wise, Seeing the world
through different eyes.
From kid to tween, a path so bright, Filled with wonder,
joy, and light.

Embracing the changes, facing the fears, Building
memories that last for years.

A journey of growth, a beautiful scene, From kid to tween, a life serene.

17. My Bestie and I

Through laughter and tears, we stand side by side, In
moments of joy, our hearts open wide.
But sometimes we argue, and tempers may flare, Yet
friendship's bond is beyond compare.

We talk it out, and make amends, For true friendship
never ends.
Through fights and makeup, our bond stays strong,
Together we belong, where we always belong.

18. Studies and Exams

Books and notes, a daily grind, Seeking knowledge,
expanding the mind.
Late-night cramming, eyes so weary, Dreams of success,
never dreary.
Exams approach, the pressure's high, But with hard
work, we'll reach the sky.
Through challenges faced, we'll stand tall, For in our
hearts, we give it our all.
Lessons learned, wisdom gained, Through effort and
focus, goals attained.
With perseverance, we'll find our way,
And celebrate success on exam day.

19. Gadgets and Games

In a world of screens, where gadgets gleam, Lost in
pixels, a digital dream.
Games and gadgets, a thrilling ride, But sometimes they
take us far and wide.
Hours pass by, eyes fixed on the screen, In virtual
worlds, where we've never been.
Challenges faced, victories won, But real-life moments,
sometimes undone.
Balance is key, in this tech-filled space, Finding time for
life's embrace.
Games and gadgets, fun and bright, But let's not forget
the world outside.

With moderation, we can enjoy, Both digital fun and
life's true joy.
For in the end, it's all about, Living fully, without a
doubt.

20. Dreams

In the heart of a ten-year-old girl, dreams take flight,
With hopes and wishes, shining so bright.
She dreams of badminton, swift and strong, Playing with
friends, where she belongs.
Colouring and drawing, her creative delight, Bringing
her imagination to life, day and night.
Speeches to give, with confidence and grace, Sharing her
thoughts, in every place.
Dancing to music, moving so free, Expressing herself,
joyfully.
Movie nights with friends, laughter and cheer, Creating
memories, year after year.
In the dreams of a ten-year-old girl, magic is found, With
endless possibilities all around.
For in her heart, a world so grand, Where dreams come
true, just as planned.

21. Pizza , Pasta , Noodles &&..

Pizza, pasta, noodles, oh what a delight, Each bite a joy, morning, noon, and night.
Pizza with toppings, so cheesy and grand, A slice of heaven, right in your hand.

Pasta so tender, with sauces divine, A taste of Italy, in every line.
Noodles so slurpy, a joy to eat, A bowl of comfort, a savory treat.

From pizza's crust to pasta's twirl, Noodles' dance, a culinary whirl.
Each bite a journey, a taste so fine, Pizza, pasta, noodles, simply sublime.

And to end the meal, a sweet surprise, Choco pudding, a treat for the eyes. Rich and creamy, a dessert so sweet, A perfect finish, a delightful treat.

That's Me - Signing off - Anshu